FINGERPRINT CHARACTERS

by Bobbie Nuytten

PICTURE WINDOW BOOKS

a capstone imprint

Welcome to the fun world of fingerprint art!

Make your own fun and silly characters with your fingers! Did you know that a fingerprint can be the start of a piece of art? Use the following pages to help you make your character creations!

Here's what you'll need to get started:

ink

Use an ink pad that's labeled washable. You can pick any size or shape you like. You can even use your favorite color!

pens

Find a pen or marker with a fine tip. An artist pen from a craft store will work too. Use the pen to add shapes and lines to your fingerprints.

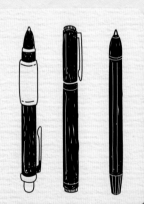

paper

Pick the paper you like best. Smooth computer paper will show the lines in your fingerprints. You can also use thicker paper from a craft store.

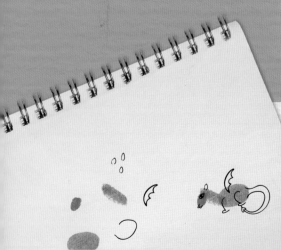

FINGERPRINT TIPS

Use different parts of your finger to change the character's size and shape.

Use the center of your finger or thumb to make oval shapes with lots of lines.

Use the tip of your finger to make small round shapes. Try using the side of your pinky finger for really small shapes.

Use the side of your finger to make long, skinny shapes.

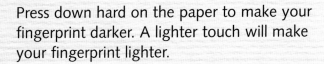

Press down hard on the paper to make your fingerprint darker. A lighter touch will make your fingerprint lighter.

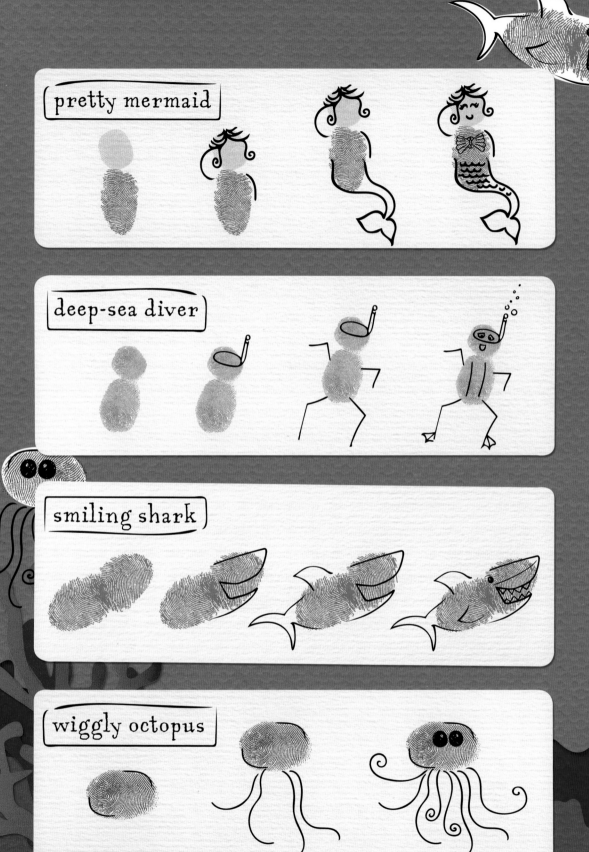

pretty mermaid

deep-sea diver

smiling shark

wiggly octopus

daring pirate

deadly Kraken

happy monkey

sneaky crocodile

long-necked dinosaur

spiky dinosaur

baby dinosaur

toothy dinosaur

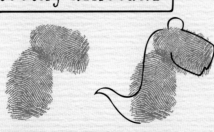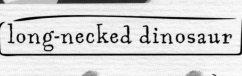

spooky ghost

moaning mummy

biting vampire bat

Frankenstein's monster

sunny flower

cutie pie bug

cheerful mushroom

happy cloud

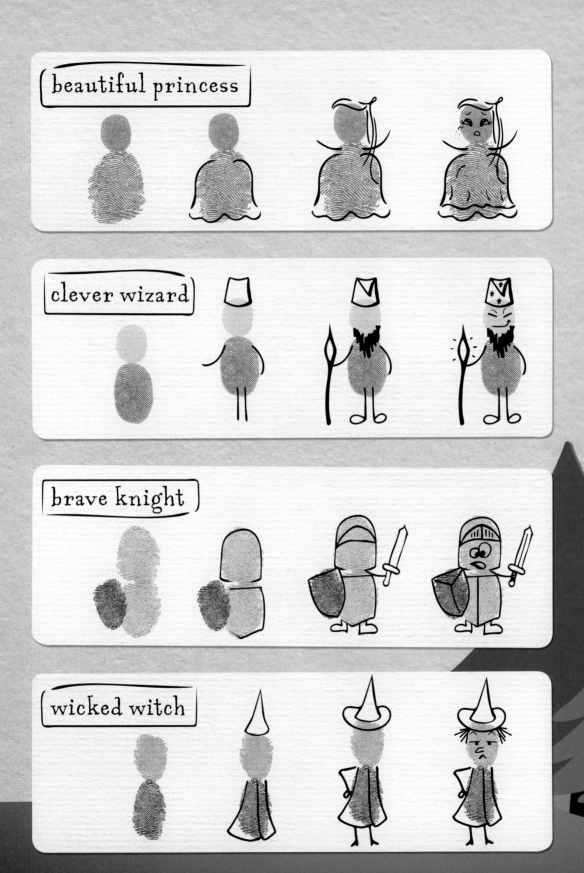

beautiful princess

clever wizard

brave knight

wicked witch

14

scaly monster

silly creature

bug-eyed monster

mighty King Kong

magical fairy

scary cyclops

prancing unicorn

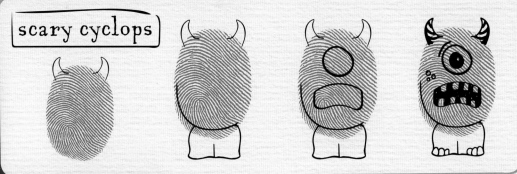

resting dragon

sweet cupcake

lovely lollypop

yummy ice-cream cone

juicy cherry

22

For Lexi and Mia—you taught me to see masterpieces in every scribble.

About the Illustrator

Bobbie Nuytten lives in southern Minnesota with her husband, two young daughters, two golden retrievers, and cat. She has been a designer for over 14 years, focusing on children's books for the last 12 years. Bobbie has always been an avid crafter. In recent years she has been interested in making art and crafts accessible and fun for kids, especially her daughters.

Read More

Bergin, Mark. *It's Fun to Draw Ghosts and Ghouls.* New York: Sky Pony Press, 2014.

Bolte, Mari. *Drawing Monsters: A Step-by-Step Sketchbook.* My First Sketchbook. North Mankato, Minn.: Capstone Press, 2015.

Florian, Douglas. *How to Draw a Dragon.* New York: Beach Lane Books, 2015.

Internet Sites

FactHound offers a safe, fun way to find Internet sites related to this book. All of the sites on FactHound have been researched by our staff.

Here's all you do:

Visit *www.facthound.com*

Type in this code: 9781479586851

Super-cool stuff! Check out projects, games and lots more at **www.capstonekids.com**

Editor: Michelle Hasselius
Designer: Bobbie Nuytten
Creative Director: Nathan Gassman
Production Specialist: Lori Blackwell

The illustrations in this book were created with pen and ink, and digital collage.

Picture Window Books are published by Capstone,
1710 Roe Crest Drive, North Mankato, Minnesota 56003
www.mycapstone.com

Library of Congress Cataloging-in-Publication Data
Cataloging-in-publication information is on file with the Library of Congress.
ISBN 978-1-4795-8685-1 (library binding)
ISBN 978-1-4795-8689-9 (eBook PDF)

Photographs and background elements from Shutterstock.

Printed in the United States of America in North Mankato, Minnesota.
102015   009221CGS16

Look for all four titles to find more ways to have fun with fingerprints!